DOPAMINE

The dark side of pleasure

Copyright

Have you ever found yourself binging a series without being able to stop watching?

Or perhaps you were mesmerized by a film that touched your emotions in a profound way?

Our brain has a habit of involving us with a special power, capable of transporting us to imaginary worlds and awakening a multitude of emotions.

But have you ever stopped to ask yourself how this happens?

In this material, we will explore the secrets behind the best approaches to neuroscience and dopamine, unveiling the strategies that scientists and researchers use to capture our attention and immerse us in a fascinating world of brain knowledge.

A brief introduction

In the human experience, the incessant search for pleasure is a powerful current that drags us towards an infinite number of tempting stimuli. From drugs to food, from social media to gambling, from shopping to casual encounters, we are surrounded by opportunities to experience pleasure at any time. But as we indulge in this insatiable pursuit, a fundamental question arises: are we truly becoming happier, or are we falling into an immediate gratification trap that keeps us from true satisfaction?

In this material, we will explore the complex interaction between the search for pleasure and the functioning of dopamine in our brain. Let's uncover what's behind this chemical and examine how it's at the heart of our relentless pursuit of pleasure. Along the way, we'll consider the implications of this cycle of immediate gratification on our mental health, well-being, and

pursuit of genuine happiness.

The Discovery of Dopamine

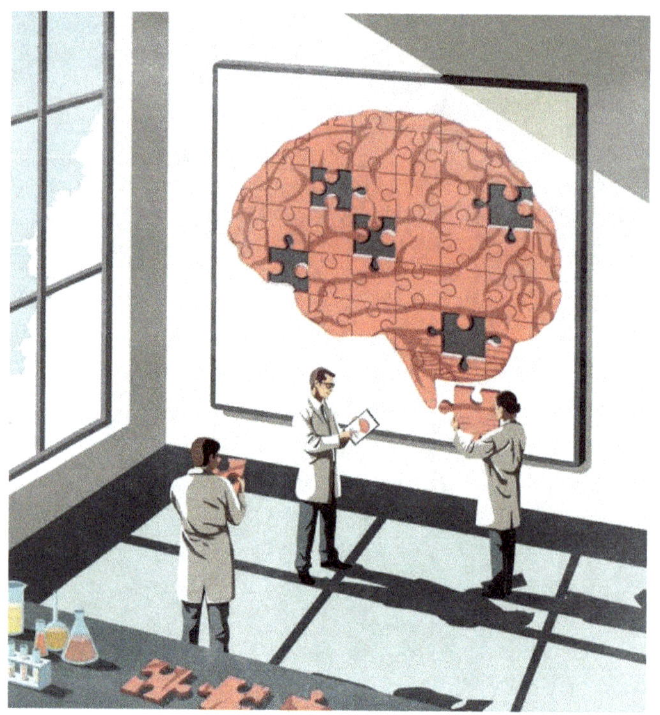

The story of dopamine begins in the 1950s, when understanding of how the brain works and the role of neurotransmitters was just beginning to develop. It was during this period that Swedish scientist Arvid Carlsson made a revolutionary discovery that shed light on one of the most important neurotransmitters in the central nervous system: dopamine.

Arvid Carlsson was born in 1923 in Uppsala, Sweden, and completed his doctorate in medicine in 1951 at Lund University. His scientific career began to take off when he joined the Department of Pharmacology at the University of Gothenburg. It was there that he began investigating the nervous system and came across an intriguing chemical known at the time as "substance H."

In 1957, Arvid Carlsson and his colleagues were able to isolate and identify this substance as a separate molecule and named it "dopamine." This name was derived from the Greek word "dopamine," which means "provoking action." The discovery of dopamine was a significant milestone in neurochemical research, as it represented the first time that a specific neurotransmitter had been successfully isolated and identified.

Dopamine, in particular, caught Carlsson's attention because of its role in motor control. He noted that dopamine was concentrated in specific areas of the brain, such as the substantia nigra, and that its lack was linked to movement disorders such as Parkinson's disease. From these observations, Carlsson began to further explore the role of dopamine in the nervous system.

His pioneering research was not just limited to identifying dopamine, but also included studies on how this chemical influenced the brain and behavior. Carlsson demonstrated that dopamine was an essential neurotransmitter for communication between neurons and played a crucial role in several functions, including mood regulation, motivation, and reward processing.

Arvid Carlsson's work has laid the foundation for understanding the complex chemical interactions that occur in the brain and how these interactions affect our mental and physical health. His pioneering spirit and dedication to research in the area of dopamine eventually led him to receive one of the most prestigious scientific awards in the world: the Nobel Prize in Physiology or Medicine.

In 2000, Arvid Carlsson was awarded the Nobel Prize, along with scientists Paul Greengard and Eric Kandel, for their contributions to understanding the mechanisms of action of neurotransmitters, including dopamine. The Nobel Prize recognized the importance of his discoveries for neuroscience and medicine, highlighting dopamine as a central component in the regulation of the human brain and mind.

The Role of Dopamine in the Brain:

A Detailed Analysis

Dopamine is a crucial neurotransmitter in the nervous system, playing multiple complex and interconnected roles in the human brain. To understand in depth the role of dopamine, it is necessary to analyze its functions in different brain areas and systems:

1. Reward System:

One of the best-known and studied roles of dopamine is its function in the brain's reward system. This system is responsible for evaluating experiences as rewarding and reinforcing behaviors that lead to these rewards.

The nucleus accumbens, a region of the brain, is central to this process. When a person experiences something pleasurable, such as eating a delicious meal or receiving compliments, neurons in this area release dopamine. This creates a feeling of motivation and satisfaction, encouraging repetition of the action that led to the reward. Dopamine acts as an "anticipated pleasure signal," motivating us to seek rewards and form habits.

However, this reward system can be exploited in negative ways, leading to addictive behaviors. Drugs, gambling, and other activities that stimulate the release of dopamine can create addiction, as the brain repeatedly seeks the feeling of pleasure associated with these substances or behaviors.

2. Mood Regulation:

In addition to the reward system, dopamine plays a key role in mood regulation. Adequate dopamine levels are associated with feelings of well-being, joy and motivation. A lack of dopamine, on the other hand, may be related to depression and other mood disorders.

In disorders such as depression, there may be a dysfunction in the regulation of dopamine, resulting in low levels of this neurotransmitter. This can contribute to symptoms such as apathy, lack of motivation and deep sadness. Antidepressant medications, such as selective serotonin and dopamine reuptake inhibitors (SRIs), target increased dopamine levels in the brain to help alleviate depressive symptoms.

3. Movement Control:

Dopamine plays a vital role in controlling movement. This function is especially evident in the substantia nigra region, located at the base of the brain. The lack of dopamine in this area is the main characteristic of Parkinson's disease.

In Parkinson's disease, the progressive death of dopamine-producing neurons in the substantia nigra results in motor symptoms such as tremors, muscle rigidity, and coordination difficulties. Standard treatment for Parkinson's disease involves medications, such as levodopa, which are converted to dopamine in the brain to compensate for the deficiency.

4. Learning and Memory:

Dopamine plays an interesting role in learning and the formation of memories, especially those associated with rewards. When you experience something rewarding, like praise or a tasty dish, the release of dopamine helps strengthen the connections between the neurons involved in forming that memory.

These reward-associated memories can influence your future behavior. For example, if you associate a specific activity with a feeling of pleasure due to the release of dopamine, you will be more likely to repeat that activity.

5. Decision Making and Motivation:

Dopamine plays a crucial role in decision making, evaluating risks and rewards, and motivation. When you face a choice, your brain evaluates the possible rewards and risks associated with each option.

The release of dopamine helps signal which options are most rewarding, influencing your final decision. This process is also related to motivation, as dopamine motivates you to pursue activities that promise rewards.

6. Reactions to Stress:

Dopamine also plays a role in the stress response system. During stressful situations, dopamine release may increase to help mobilize energy and attention to deal with the perceived threat. However, in chronic cases of stress, dysfunction in dopamine regulation may be related to disorders such as post-traumatic stress disorder (PTSD).

Dopamine is an incredibly versatile neurotransmitter that plays a number of critical roles in the human brain. Its influence extends from the reward system, where it motivates pleasure-seeking and habit formation, to mood regulation, movement control, learning and memory, decision-making, motivation, and even reactions to stress.

As neuroscientific research continues to advance, our knowledge of dopamine and its influence on human behavior also deepens, opening the door to new therapies and interventions.

Dopamine in the Gastrointestinal Tract: An Intriguing Revelation

The discovery of dopamine outside the brain, specifically in the gastrointestinal tract, brought to light a new dimension in understanding how this molecule affects our body. The presence of dopamine in the gastrointestinal tract was initially identified in the 1970s and 1980s, and has since been the subject of intense research.

The gastrointestinal tract, or digestive system, is made up of a complex set of organs, including the stomach, small intestine, and large intestine. Its main function is the digestion of food and the absorption of nutrients essential for the functioning of the body. However, it is also a system highly regulated by the nervous system, and dopamine plays a key role in this regulation.

The Hidden Power of Dopamine in Romantic Love: How Brain Chemistry Influences Our Emotions

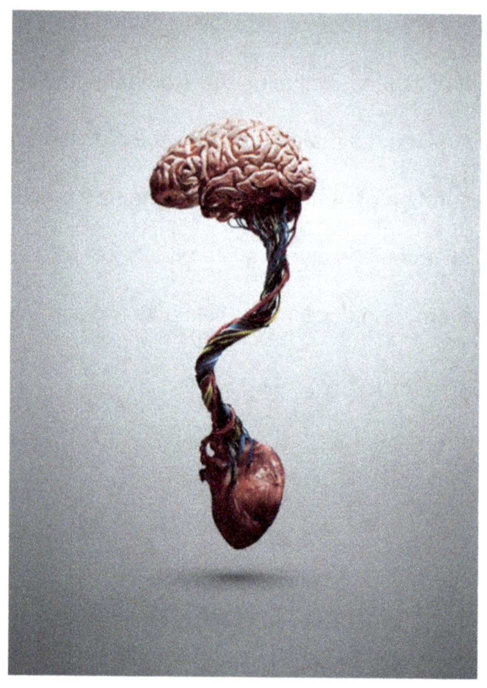

Love is one of the deepest and most mysterious human experiences. It's a feeling that has inspired poets, artists, and philosophers throughout history, and has often been described as an overwhelming, inexplicable force. However, modern science has shed light on the mechanisms underlying love, revealing that dopamine, a brain chemical, plays a crucial role in initiating and maintaining romantic love.

Imagine that magical moment when you meet someone special and feel a spark of intense attraction. Your heart races, your hands sweat, and you feel an overwhelming sense of happiness. This sensation, known as "butterflies in the stomach", is a complex biochemical response, and dopamine is one of the protagonists of this emotional scenario.

The Beginning of Romantic Love: Dopamine in Action

When you meet someone who piques your romantic interest, your brain goes into overdrive. An area of the brain known as the nucleus accumbens, which is part of the reward system, is activated. At this point, dopamine begins to be released at higher levels than normal. This burst of dopamine is responsible for the feeling of euphoria and excitement that often accompanies the beginning of a romantic relationship.

Dopamine acts as a chemical messenger that signals to the brain the importance of the stimulus you are experiencing. In other words, it makes you feel good in the presence of the person you love, encouraging you to spend more time with them and seek a deeper connection. This is why, at the beginning of romantic love, many of us feel an irresistible attraction, a constant need to be close to our loved one, and an intense desire to create a deeper emotional connection.

The Maintenance of Romantic Love: Dopamine as an Ally

As the romantic relationship progresses and the initial phase of intense passion subsides, dopamine continues to play a vital role in maintaining romantic love. Although the initial euphoria may subside, the constant presence of dopamine helps maintain the emotional bond between partners.

Dopamine is involved in the formation of memories associated with rewards. This means that the happy moments you share with your partner, the affectionate gestures, the laughter and the heartwarming experiences are all registered in your brain with the help of dopamine. These positive memories strengthen your relationship and create a sense of reward whenever you are with your partner.

Additionally, dopamine is linked to desire and motivation. It encourages us to make efforts to maintain and improve the relationship. It motivates us to be affectionate, to resolve conflicts and to invest time and energy in our partner. The feeling of gratification we feel when we do something to please our partner is, in part, a result of the action of dopamine.

Challenges of Romantic Love: When Dopamine Comes into Play

While dopamine is a powerful ally in romantic love, it can also present challenges. The same reward system that makes us feel so good when we're in love can make us vulnerable to intense feelings of sadness and anxiety when the relationship struggles.

For example, in a breakup, the lack of a loved one's constant presence can lead to a drop in dopamine levels, resulting in withdrawal symptoms similar to those experienced by people quitting drugs. The deep sadness and feeling of emptiness after the end of a relationship can be explained, in part, by the drop in dopamine levels.

The Power of Understanding Dopamine in Romantic Love

Understanding the role of dopamine in romantic love not only gives us deeper insight into our emotions, but can also help us better navigate the challenges of romantic relationships. Knowing that the initial intensity of passion is largely a result of the action of dopamine allows us to fully appreciate it while understanding that it can lessen over time.

Additionally, dopamine reminds us of the importance of investing in our relationship, creating positive memories, and keeping the flame of love alive. The knowledge that dopamine is involved in the formation of memories associated with rewards encourages us to create special moments with our partner, strengthening emotional bonds.

In short, dopamine is one of the driving forces behind romantic love. It makes us feel alive, passionate and motivated to seek deep connections with our partners. Understanding the role of this chemical in our emotions helps us value the experience of romantic love even more and face the challenges that may arise along the way. Love is an incredible journey, and dopamine is one of our greatest allies on this wonderful journey. So open your heart, let the dopamine flow, and enjoy the magic of romantic love.

Dopamine in the Gastrointestinal Tract:

Functions and Impact on Health

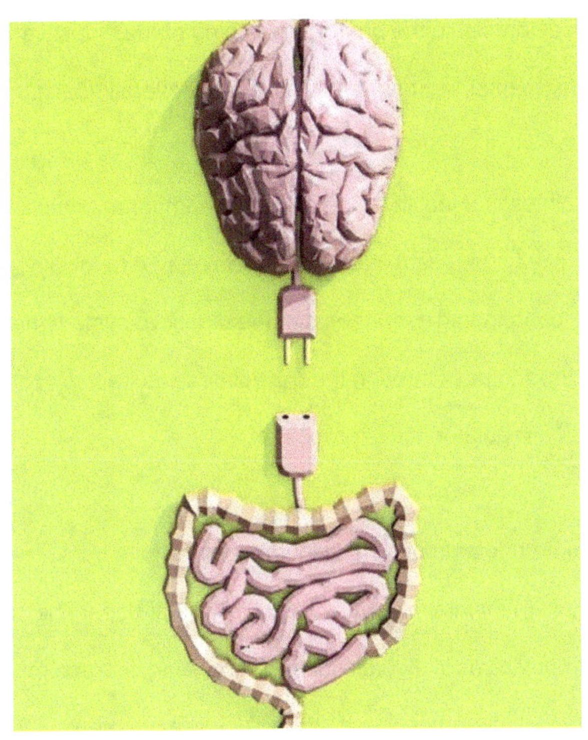

Dopamine in the gastrointestinal tract performs several functions crucial to the proper functioning of the digestive system and has important implications for overall health.

Gastrointestinal Motility: One of the most important functions of dopamine in the gastrointestinal tract is related to motility, that is, the coordinated movements of the digestive system that allow food to pass through the gastrointestinal tract. Dopamine acts as a regulator of this process.

Adequate dopamine levels in the gastrointestinal tract are essential to maintain normal motility. A lack of dopamine can lead to problems like constipation, a condition characterized by slow bowel movements and difficult bowel movements. On the other hand, an excess of dopamine can result in excessively rapid motility, leading to diarrhea.

Gastric Acid Production: Another important function of dopamine in the gastrointestinal tract is related to the regulation of gastric acid production in the stomach. Gastric acid is essential for digesting food and destroying unwanted bacteria. Dopamine acts as a modulator of this process.

Adequate levels of dopamine in the stomach ensure the controlled production of gastric acid, allowing proper digestion of food. However, imbalances in dopamine regulation can result in excessive or insufficient production of stomach acid, leading to problems such as heartburn, acid reflux and indigestion.

Feeling of Nausea: Dopamine is also involved in regulating the feeling of nausea. When an irritation occurs in the gastrointestinal tract, such as eating contaminated food, dopamine can be released in response to this stimulus. This triggers the feeling of nausea, which serves as a protective mechanism to prevent further ingestion of potentially harmful substances.

Impact on Gastrointestinal Disorders: Imbalances in dopamine regulation in the gastrointestinal tract have been associated with a number of gastrointestinal disorders. For example, in Parkinson's disease, which is characterized by the degeneration of dopamine-producing neurons, the motor symptoms are well known, but gastrointestinal problems such as constipation can also occur.

Additionally, dopamine is implicated in disorders such as irritable bowel syndrome (IBS) and gastroparesis. In IBS, imbalances in dopamine regulation can contribute to symptoms such as abdominal pain, bloating, and irregularities in bowel movements. Gastroparesis, in turn, is a condition in which the stomach does not empty properly, and dopamine plays a role in regulating gastric motility.

Dopamine and Communication between the Brain and the Gastrointestinal Tract: One of the most intriguing discoveries is the existence of a bidirectional communication between the brain and the gastrointestinal tract, mediated in part by dopamine. This means the brain can affect gastrointestinal function and vice versa.

When we are stressed, anxious, or emotionally upset, the brain can send signals that affect gastrointestinal motility and function. This is one of the reasons why many people experience gastrointestinal upset in situations of stress or anxiety. Dopamine plays a role in this communication, influencing emotional responses that can affect the functioning of the gastrointestinal tract.

The Role of Dopamine in Enteroendocrine Cells: A recent discovery that has gained prominence in research is the role of dopamine in the enteroendocrine cells of the gastrointestinal tract. These cells play a crucial role in regulating food intake and producing hormones involved in appetite control.

Dopamine produced by enteroendocrine cells acts as a regulator in the release of hormones, such as ghrelin (hunger hormone) and leptin (satiety hormone). This means that dopamine not only influences digestion, but can also affect our feelings of hunger and satiety.

Therapeutic Implications: The increasing understanding of the role of dopamine in the gastrointestinal tract has promising therapeutic implications. Researchers are exploring ways to modulate dopamine levels in the gastrointestinal tract to treat disorders such as chronic constipation, IBS, and gastroparesis. Furthermore, understanding this complex communication network between the brain and the gastrointestinal tract could lead to more integrated approaches to treating eating disorders and obesity.

Dopamine, a molecule famous for its role in the brain, turns out to be an equally important and complex figure in the gastrointestinal tract. Its presence and regulation are crucial for

the proper functioning of the digestive system and have
significant implications for overall health.

Understanding the functions of dopamine in the gastrointestinal
tract is constantly evolving, and additional research is needed
to fully clarify its mechanisms and therapeutic potential.
However, this expansion of our knowledge about dopamine
leads us to a deeper appreciation of the complexity of the
human body and the fascinating interactions between different
organ systems. As research continues, we can expect new
discoveries to reveal even more about dopamine's multifaceted
role in our health and well-being.

The Neurochemical Dance of Dopamine and Tyrosine

To fully understand the relationship between tyrosine and dopamine, it's important to take a look at the neurochemical dance that takes place in our brain. Dopamine is synthesized in several regions of the brain, but its primary source is the substantia nigra, a structure in the central part of the brain. Dopamine synthesis begins with tyrosine, which is converted to L-DOPA by an enzyme called tyrosine hydroxylase. L-DOPA is then converted into dopamine by the enzyme dopa-decarboxylase.

Dopamine is essential for the normal functioning of the nervous system, and adequate availability of tyrosine is a critical factor in this process. Without enough tyrosine, the body cannot produce dopamine in adequate amounts, which can lead to a number of neurochemical imbalances.

Tyrosine, often called "precursor tyrosine," is obtained from the diet and is also synthesized by the body from another amino acid, phenylalanine. It is present in a variety of foods, such as meat, fish, eggs, dairy products, nuts, seeds and legumes. When tyrosine is absorbed by the body or synthesized from phenylalanine, it becomes a vital link in the dopamine production chain.

Tyrosine deficiency can have serious consequences for dopamine synthesis and, in turn, mental and physical health. In rare cases, phenylketonuria, a genetic disease, prevents the proper conversion of phenylalanine to tyrosine, leading to a tyrosine deficiency. This can cause mental retardation and serious neurological problems if left untreated.

Maintaining a balanced diet that includes sources of tyrosine is essential to ensure that the body has the necessary precursor for the production of dopamine. By understanding the connection between tyrosine and dopamine, we can appreciate how our food choices and health care can profoundly affect our

brain function and emotional well-being. Therefore, do not

underestimate the fundamental role played by tyrosine.

The Reward System

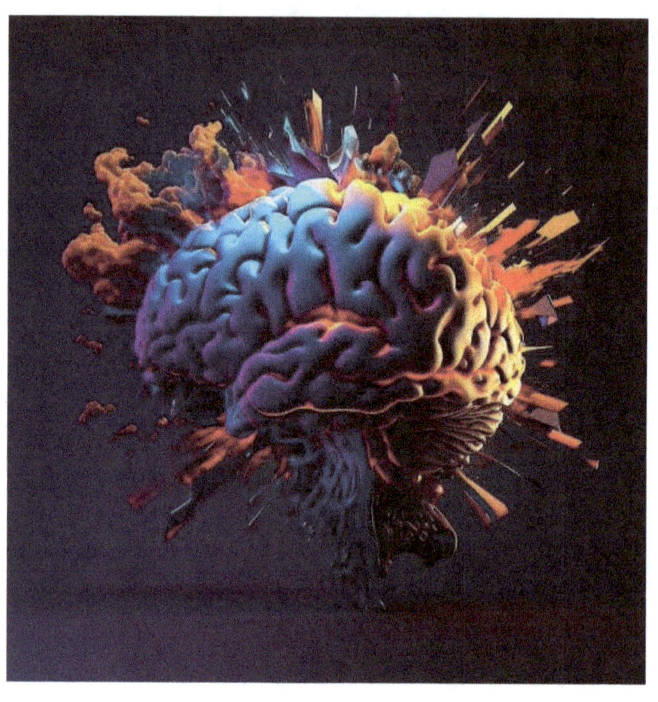

Did you know that a part of your brain plays a key role in creating motivation and influencing the way we face challenging behaviors, like that dreaded Monday?

I'm talking about the reward system, it is made up of several brain structures and interconnected neural networks that play a crucial role in generating behaviors related to motivation and pleasure. It is important to highlight that reward is related to learning the value of a behavior, while pleasure is associated with liking or feeling good when performing that behavior.

This system uses positive aspects of emotions, such as pleasure and desires, to create the motivation necessary to perform specific behaviors. For example, not all behaviors need to be intrinsically pleasurable to be related to reward activity. Some behaviors, such as work, may not provide immediate pleasure, but we learn to be motivated to perform them, as we recognize the need to earn money to achieve the things we enjoy.

The reward system is composed of several brain regions, including the ventral tegmental area, nucleus accumbens, striatum, prefrontal cortex, anterior cingulate cortex, hippocampus, hypothalamus, and amygdala. Each of these regions plays a specific role in the cognitive processing of this system, contributing to our motivation towards specific behaviors.

Dopamine is an essential neurotransmitter for controlling the activity of the reward system. It is produced in the ventral tegmental area and projects to several other areas of the reward system. Dopaminergic activity in the ventral tegmental area activates the nucleus accumbens, spreading activation throughout the reward system. This pathway is known as the mesolimbic dopaminergic pathway.

To understand how the processing of the reward system works, we can consider the example of eating a bar of milk chocolate for the first time. Your brain identifies that you are eating something highly tasty due to the levels of sugar and fat present in the bar. As a result, the activity of the mesolimbic pathway is activated, leading to an increase in dopamine release. The nucleus accumbens communicates with the amygdala to identify the emotion associated with eating chocolate, which is pleasure. This communication helps the hippocampus form a memory that associates eating chocolate with pleasure, creating motivation to repeat this behavior.

It is important to note that the reward system is not limited to intrinsically pleasurable behaviors. Behaviors that may not be naturally pleasurable, such as work, can become motivating when we associate earning money with achieving our personal goals and pleasures. This is because the brain predicts the feeling of pleasure or the achievement of goals through this work.

Furthermore, several psychiatric disorders can affect the reward system, dysregulating specific parts of the neural network. This can result in symptoms such as anhedonia in depression, lack of motivation and interest in carrying out activities, and in other disorders such as ADHD, schizophrenia, bipolar disorder, anxiety disorder and depressive disorders.

Addictive drugs also have the ability to hyperactivate the mesolimbic dopaminergic pathway, hijacking the reward system. This leads to excessive motivation to obtain more drugs, often to the detriment of normal daily activities.

In short, the reward system, with dopamine as its centerpiece, plays a key role in our motivation, learning, habit formation, and decision-making. It drives us to seek activities that result in rewards and pleasure, shaping our behavior and influencing our choices. Understanding how dopamine and the reward system work is essential to understanding our drives, behaviors, and the challenges faced by those with psychiatric disorders or addictions. Dopamine is not just a neurotransmitter; it is a key to unlocking the mysteries of motivation and pleasure that shape our lives.

The Prefrontal Cortex - The Brain Command Tower

One of the characteristics that distinguishes us from other animals, even from primates closest in our evolution, is the development and complexity of the functioning of a brain region called the prefrontal cortex. In this material you will understand what the prefrontal cortex is, the different areas that make it up and their importance for different brain functions.

The prefrontal cortex plays a crucial role in several functions, from planning and executing actions to controlling our behaviors.

It gets its name because it is located in the frontal lobe of the brain and can be subdivided into five distinct areas: lateral dorsum, medial dorsum, lateral belly, medial belly and frontal orbit.

All of these areas are connected to other parts of the brain, such as the association areas and the limbic system.

The prefrontal cortex is vital for essential cognitive functions known as executive control or executive functions. This includes cognitive processes fundamental to controlling our behavior, such as attention, inhibitory control, working memory, cognitive flexibility, reasoning, planning and problem solving. These functions play a significant role in our intelligence and our ability to interact socially.

In fact, many consider the prefrontal cortex to be a kind of "command tower" for our personality and behavior. Its complexity and capacity have led to our ability to develop technologies and scientific advances.

One way we began to understand the importance of the prefrontal cortex was through the famous case of Phineas Gage, a construction worker who suffered an accident in which

an iron bar passed through part of his prefrontal cortex.
Changes in its behavior allowed us to understand the functions
of this region.

With advances in neuroscience, we have attempted to identify
specific functions within the prefrontal cortex related to specific
areas, such as the dorsolateral prefrontal cortex, which appears
to be involved in processes of verbal fluency and thought
organization. This area is particularly important for working
memory, which is essential for maintaining verbal fluency and
flow of thoughts during speaking and reading.

The ventral medial area, on the other hand, is associated with
both working memory and decision making. It plays a
fundamental role when you are evaluating whether or not to
make a decision, weighing the consequences and rewards of
the action.

The orbitofrontal prefrontal cortex has a deep connection with our emotional states and influences our decisions based on our emotional and ethical values. It is capable of mediating our personality, decision-making and emotions, using the hypothesis of somatic markers, as discussed by Antonio Damásio in his book "Descartes' Error".

Although many studies have attempted to map specific functions to specific areas of the prefrontal cortex, the current consensus is that all areas play roles in diverse executive functions, with no clear and exclusive separation of functions in specific areas. The complexity and interconnectedness of executive functions make the prefrontal cortex essential to our intelligence, personality, and social functioning.

Studies also reveal that dysfunctions in the prefrontal cortex are associated with several psychiatric and neurodevelopmental disorders, such as ADHD, anxiety, depression and bipolar disorder, negatively affecting cognitive and emotional functions.

SEROTONIN = HAPPINESS?

You may have heard about serotonin as the 'happy hormone', something that perhaps explains why eating chocolate can make us feel good, as it increases serotonin levels.

However, is this the only role of this neurotransmitter in our brain?

I want to address the different functions of serotonin, explaining how it is absorbed in our body, synthesized and its relationship with disorders such as anxiety and depression. To begin with, it is important to understand what serotonin is.

Serotonin is a neurotransmitter released by synapses in our brain.

Interestingly, although it is essential for brain function, around ninety percent of serotonin is produced and remains in our intestines, specifically in enterochromaffin cells.

In biochemical terms, serotonin results from reactions that involve tryptophan, transforming it into 5-hydroxytryptophan and then into 5-hydroxytryptamine, also known as serotonin or 5-HTP.

As mentioned, serotonin in the intestine is produced in response to food stimuli, increasing intestinal motility. However, in addition to its function in the intestine, serotonin plays an essential role in regulating various behaviors. There are specific areas of the brain that contain neurons that release serotonin, known as serotonergic neurons. These neurons project to various parts of the brain, including the prefrontal cortex and other areas important for the various functions that serotonin performs.

It is crucial to understand that whenever serotonin is released by a neuron, it acts like any other neurotransmitter, interacting with receptor proteins. Currently, it is known that there are more than 14 different types of serotonin receptors, each expressed in different areas of the brain and responsible for regulating specific functions.

One of the most studied functions of serotonin is its relationship with aggression and impulsivity. Studies indicate that a decrease in the activity of specific serotonin receptors is linked to an increase in these behaviors. However, there is controversy, as other studies suggest the opposite, that increases in serotonin levels can increase aggression. Therefore, the correlation between serotonin levels and these behaviors is not yet completely understood.

Another important function is the regulation of serotonin in anxiety disorders. Research has shown that serotonin plays a vital role in modulating responses to stressful stimuli, making us more tolerant of them.

Decreased serotonin levels appear to make people more sensitive to these stressful stimuli, while taking antidepressants that increase serotonin can reduce anxiety.

Serotonin regulation is also related to mood, and studies have shown that low levels of serotonin can contribute to depression. On the other hand, increasing serotonin levels through antidepressants can improve mood.

Have more or less dopamine?

Having more or less dopamine in your central nervous system is not a matter of "good" or "bad" in a general sense, as dopamine plays crucial roles in several bodily functions. The assessment of whether it is preferable to have more or less dopamine depends on the context, individual health and a person's specific needs.

Having more dopamine can be beneficial in certain cases:

Motivation and reward: Dopamine is associated with the feeling of reward and motivation. Having adequate dopamine levels can help maintain motivation to perform tasks and achieve goals.

Emotional well-being: Dopamine plays a role in mood and feelings of pleasure. Having balanced dopamine levels is important to avoid symptoms of depression and anxiety.

Cognitive functions: Dopamine is involved in cognitive functions such as attention, concentration and short-term memory. Having adequate dopamine levels may be important for cognitive performance.

However, having too much dopamine can lead to problems like:

Addictive behaviors: Dopamine is related to addiction, as the constant search for rewards can lead to addictive behaviors such as gambling, excessive substance use, and binge eating.

Psychiatric disorders: Abnormally high levels of dopamine are associated with neuropsychiatric disorders such as schizophrenia and bipolar disorder.

Risky behaviors: People with high dopamine levels may engage in risky behaviors, such as dangerous driving and extreme sensation seeking.

On the other hand, having less dopamine can also be problematic:

Reduced motivation: Low dopamine levels can lead to a lack of motivation, apathy, and difficulty pursuing goals.

Depressive symptoms: Decreased dopamine is associated with depression and anhedonia, a condition in which people lose the ability to feel pleasure.

Concentration issues: Dopamine plays a role in attention and concentration, so low levels can negatively affect these functions.

Balancing dopamine levels is essential for physical and mental well-being. It's not a matter of having "more" or "less" dopamine, but rather maintaining healthy, balanced levels to meet individual needs and avoid mental and behavioral health problems. The regulation of dopamine levels should be done by healthcare professionals, when necessary, and not on your own.

The Risk of Dopamine Imbalance

Although dopamine is essential for our motivation and pleasure, an imbalance in its levels can lead to serious problems, including addiction. When activities or substances that release dopamine are used in excess, the brain can adapt, resulting in the need for increasingly larger doses to experience the same levels of pleasure. This creates a vicious cycle that can lead to addiction.

Addiction can take many forms, from substances such as alcohol, tobacco and illicit drugs to behaviors such as gambling, compulsive shopping, pornography and excessive use of technology. In all of these cases, dopamine plays a central role in the relentless pursuit of rewards.

Now that we understand the importance of dopamine and the risks associated with its imbalance, let's explore strategies to regulate dopamine in a healthy way and reduce the risk of addiction:

1. Awareness

The first step to avoiding addiction is to be aware of risk factors and how dopamine works. Understanding that activities or substances that provide excessive pleasure can lead to problems is essential.

2. Establishing Limits

Setting limits is crucial to avoiding addiction. This involves establishing rules for using substances or participating in behaviors that release dopamine. For example, set time limits for using social media or video games.

3. Diversification of Sources of Pleasure

Instead of relying on a single source of pleasure, it's important to diversify your activities and interests. This reduces the

likelihood of becoming overly dependent on a single source of
dopamine.

4. Physical Exercise

Regular physical activity can naturally increase dopamine
levels in the brain, providing a feeling of well-being. Exercise is
a healthy way to experience rewards and should be
incorporated into your daily routine.

5. Balanced Diet

Diet plays an important role in regulating neurotransmitters,
including dopamine. Certain nutrients, such as tyrosine and
tryptophan, are precursors to dopamine. A balanced diet that
includes foods rich in these nutrients can help maintain healthy
dopamine levels.

6. Mindfulness Practice

Meditation and mindfulness practices can help develop
emotional self-regulation and reduce the search for instant

rewards. These techniques promote awareness of the present moment and can reduce impulsivity.

7. Seeking Professional Help

If you think you are at risk of developing an addiction or are already struggling with addiction, seeking professional help is essential. Therapists, counselors, and support groups can offer valuable support in overcoming addiction.

8. Avoid the Use of Recreational Substances

The use of recreational substances, such as illicit drugs and alcohol, can quickly lead to addiction due to the significant impact they have on dopamine release. Avoiding the use of these substances is an important measure to avoid addiction.

9. Reducing the Use of Technology

Excessive use of technological devices such as smartphones and computers can lead to addiction to social media and gaming. Setting time limits for using these devices can help prevent digital addiction.

10. Positive Reinforcement

Rewarding yourself for achieving personal goals and achievements is a healthy way to release dopamine. This stimulates intrinsic motivation and reduces the need to seek external rewards.

Dopamine plays a fundamental role in our search for pleasure, motivation and well-being. However, imbalance in dopamine levels can lead to addiction to substances or behaviors. Remember that balance is key, and moderation in all areas of life is essential to maintaining a healthy relationship with dopamine.

The Serotonin and Dopamine Dilemma

Imagine yourself in an African savannah, lost and hungry. You find three juicy oranges within reach, but there is a river in front of you, and on the other side, there is an orchard full of these fruits. If your brain is flooded with dopamine, your first reaction will be, "I need the oranges on the other side!" Dopamine is the neurotransmitter of reward, driving us to seek more, always more.

Now consider the opposite: a brain with high levels of serotonin.

In this situation, you would probably think, "I have enough here." Serotonin is often associated with calm and satisfaction with what we already have. It's as if this neurotransmitter tells us that we don't need to constantly seek new rewards, that we are satisfied with what we have already achieved.

However, the key to a healthy emotional life lies not just in one or the other of these neurotransmitters, but in finding a balance between the two. This is where the concept of having a "dopaminergic" life during the day and a "serotonergic" life during the night comes in.

Dopaminergic and Serotoninergic Balance

During the day, it is natural that we seek to carry out tasks, achieve goals and seek rewards. During this period, dopamine plays a vital role, driving our actions and motivations.

On the other hand, at night, on weekends or during vacations, it is important to slow down and allow serotonin to exert its calming effect. It is in these moments that we must reflect on our achievements, appreciate what we have and move away from the incessant search for more.

The balance between these two neurotransmitters can be achieved through mindful practices, such as meditation and exercising gratitude. Meditation helps modulate brain activity, calming the areas of the limbic system responsible for anxiety. Exercising gratitude reminds us of the positive things in our lives, stimulating the release of serotonin.

Recognize, Accept, Investigate and Do Not Identify

A valuable mental exercise for achieving this emotional balance is the "Recognize, Accept, Investigate, Deidentify" method. This method, often used in cognitive therapies, helps to deal with disturbing thoughts and emotions.

Recognize: The first step is to recognize what is happening in your mind and body. This is the time to identify unwanted emotions or thoughts.

Accept: Then accept these emotions or thoughts without judgement. Do not try to deny or repress them as this can lead to denial or suppression.

Investigate: After accepting, investigate why these emotions or thoughts are present. Examine your causes and how you are reacting to them.

Don't Identify: Finally, don't identify with these emotions or thoughts. Understand that they do not define who you are, but are a natural part of the human experience.

Understanding the complex interplay between dopamine and serotonin is just the beginning. For many, the real challenge lies in reversing ingrained habits, especially those related to the incessant pursuit of dopaminergic rewards.

Just like learning a new language, modifying your behavior takes practice and patience. Neuroplasticity, the brain's ability to adapt and change, is key to this transformation. If your brain is used to operating in a high dopamine state, it will take effort and time to slow down.

Remember that changing habits and modulating dopamine levels takes patience and practice. The influence of the verbal community around you is also vital, as people can speed up or slow down your search for rewards.

Therefore, consciously seek a balance between the search for more and the appreciation of what you already have. With these practices and understanding, you will be better equipped to face life's challenges with calm and satisfaction.

The Illusion of Perfect Escape:

In Search of Eternal Happiness

The search to escape suffering is a journey that many of us undertake throughout our lives.

One of the most seductive traps in this quest is the belief in the "perfect escape", in the possibility of reaching a state of eternal happiness, where pain and discomfort are eliminated forever. This illusion, fed by representations of popular culture and by human nature itself, deserves a deeper analysis.

The Promise of Eternal Happiness

Popular culture often portrays happiness as a constant state of bliss, in which all worries and sadness are eliminated. Movies, TV shows, books and even social media often show us images of people living seemingly perfect lives, full of pleasure and joy.

These representations create the illusion that happiness can be a constant in our lives, as long as we find the right way to achieve it.

This promise of eternal happiness is seductive because it appeals directly to our innate desire to avoid suffering. No one likes to feel sad, frustrated, distressed or in pain. So it's natural for us to look for ways to escape these uncomfortable emotions. However, the question that arises is: will this quest to escape suffering really lead us to eternal happiness?

The Endless Cycle of Dissatisfaction

The fundamental problem with seeking to escape suffering is that it often puts us in an endless cycle of dissatisfaction. Here is how this cycle plays out:

Pleasure Seeking: Initially, we seek pleasure and instant gratification as a means of avoiding suffering. This may include eating delicious foods, watching exciting movies, using substances such as alcohol or drugs, or pursuing intimate relationships.

Ephemeral Pleasure: We find momentary pleasure in these activities. For a brief time, we feel good, our worries melt away, and life seems perfect.

Emotional Emptiness: However, as pleasure diminishes, we are faced with an emotional emptiness. The feeling of happiness we experience is ephemeral and fleeting. We start to feel empty, like something is missing.

Continued Search: Emotional emptiness takes us back to the search for pleasure. We believe that if we just seek more pleasure or new experiences, we will ultimately be filled with lasting happiness.

Cycle Repetition: This cycle repeats itself indefinitely. We endlessly seek pleasure, only to be repeatedly confronted with the emotional emptiness that follows. As a result, we never achieve the eternal happiness we seek.

Why is the "Perfect Escape" an Illusion?

The illusion of the "perfect escape" is harmful for several reasons:

Ephemerality of Pleasure: The ephemeral nature of pleasure means that it can never be maintained indefinitely. Even the most pleasurable experiences eventually lose their charm, leaving us feeling like something is missing.

Tolerance and Dependence: Constantly seeking pleasure can lead to tolerance, where we need increasingly larger doses to feel the same level of satisfaction. This can result in addiction to substances or harmful behaviors.

Lack of Resilience: The constant search to escape suffering can make us less emotionally resilient. When we face adversity, we may not have the necessary skills to deal with discomfort, as we are used to avoiding it.

Chronic Dissatisfaction: This cycle of incessant pursuit of pleasure can result in chronic dissatisfaction. We never feel satisfied with what we have, because we believe that the next pleasurable experience will bring us ultimate happiness.

The Importance of Acceptance and Balance

So how can we escape this cycle of dissatisfaction? A healthier approach involves practicing acceptance and finding balance. Instead of constantly seeking to escape suffering, we can learn to accept that pain and discomfort are inevitable parts of human life.

Acceptance does not mean passive resignation, but recognizing that life is made up of both pleasant and unpleasant moments. By accepting suffering as part of the human experience, we can develop emotional resilience that allows us to face challenges with more serenity.

Furthermore, it is important to seek balance in our lives. Rather than seeking constant pleasure, we can find meaning and satisfaction in a variety of experiences, including those that may involve some degree of discomfort. The search for balance allows us to live fuller and more authentic lives.

The Journey in Search of Meaning

Ultimately, the search for eternal happiness may be an illusion, but that doesn't mean we should give up on seeking happiness. Instead, we can direct our search toward meaning and purpose. Happiness is not necessarily in the absence of suffering, but in the ability to find meaning, growth and connection in the midst of difficulties.

The journey toward meaning can lead us to explore our values, develop meaningful relationships, contribute to the well-being of others, and seek a greater purpose in our lives. It is a journey that recognizes suffering as an integral part of the human condition, but also seeks to transcend that suffering through personal growth and the pursuit of what truly matters.

Embrace the Reality of Human Life. The illusion of the "perfect escape" reminds us that eternal happiness can be a fruitless pursuit. Instead of chasing a state of constant bliss, we can find meaning and satisfaction in our human journey, which includes moments of joy but also challenges and suffering.

Understand that we can accept, grow and find happiness not as a final destination, but as an ongoing journey of self-discovery and connection with the world around us. The illusion of the "perfect escape" can be left behind in favor of a richer, more authentic life where suffering is just one part of the bigger picture of existence.

Conclusion

Throughout this material, we delve deeply into the complex and fascinating world of dopamine, a fundamental neurotransmitter that plays a crucial role in our experience of pleasure, motivation, and various aspects of our everyday lives. Our journey began with an exploration of the biological basis of dopamine and how it is synthesized and released in the brain. Next, we examine how dopamine influences our behaviors, both intrinsically pleasurable and extrinsically motivated. We discuss the reward system and how it is intrinsically linked to dopamine, as well as the complex interplay between the reward system and emotions. Furthermore, we investigated the importance of the prefrontal cortex in the regulation of dopamine and its influence on executive functions and behavior control. Finally, we explore crucial questions related to dopamine regulation, addictions, and strategies for maintaining a healthy balance.

9 798861 631792